A SCHOOL SURVIVAL GUIDE

HOW TO WRITE SUPER SCHOOL REPORTS

REVISED EDITION

Elizabeth James and Carol Barkin

Beech Tree
New York

(Previous edition published as
How to Write a Great School Report)

Acknowledgment

The excerpts on pages 26, 27, and 28 are from *The Sea Otter,* by Alvin, Virginia, and Robert Silverstein. Copyright © 1995 by The Millbrook Press, Inc., and reprinted by permission of The Millbrook Press, Inc.

Published by Lothrop, Lee & Shepard Books
an imprint of Morrow Junior Books
a division of William Morrow and Company, Inc.
1350 Avenue of the Americas, New York, NY 10019
www.williammorrow.com

Printed in the United States of America.

The Library of Congress has cataloged the Lothrop, Lee & Shepard Books version of *How to Write Super School Reports* as follows:
James, Elizabeth.
How to write super school reports / by Elizabeth James and Carol Barkin.—Rev. ed.
p. cm.
Rev. ed. of: How to write a great school report. c1983.
Includes index.
Summary: Explains how to choose a topic for a report, how to find and organize information, and how to write and revise the final version.
ISBN 0-688-16132-4
1. Report writing—Juvenile literature. [1. Report writing.
2. Research.] I. Barkin, Carol. II. James, Elizabeth. How to write a great school report. III. Title. LB1047.3.J34 1998
372.13028'1—dc21   98-13767   CIP AC

Revised Beech Tree Edition, 1998
ISBN 0-688-16141-3

10 9 8 7 6 5 4 3 2

CONTENTS

CHAPTER 1

WHAT IS A REPORT?

ALMOST AS SOON AS YOU LEARN how to write, you start writing reports for school. Writing a report lets you find out more about something *you're* interested in. And it gives you the chance to say just what *you* want to say. Lots of people really like writing reports.

In third grade, you might write about your pet or about an exciting trip you took. In fifth grade, you might do a report on a video game you know a lot about or on what it's like to be a newspaper reporter. Sometimes you can write about whatever you want. But even if your teacher assigns a topic, you get to decide what part of that topic most interests you. Putting together a report lets you share what you've learned. And it's much more fun than filling in the blanks on a work sheet!

But what if you don't know how to get started? It can be scary to write something all by yourself. You may feel confused if you don't understand what to do.

A good way to begin is to figure out what a report really is. Once you get the idea, you'll be able to write a report on any topic.

A report is a collection of information about a topic. But that's not all it is. A report is a way of telling other people what you found interesting and exciting about that topic. Instead of telling them in spoken words, though, you're telling them in writing.

Of course, the information in a report must be correct. Suppose you read a report on how to bake a cake. If the directions told you to add one cup of salt and one teaspoon of sugar, that is what you would do. But your cake would taste terrible! You might be pretty mad at the person who wrote down the wrong information. Or suppose you read a social studies report that mentioned something that just happened in the USSR (Union of Soviet Socialist Republics). This country has now become several smaller countries, so the USSR doesn't exist anymore. You would know that the writer of this report didn't bother to find the correct information. And you might wonder if the rest of the facts in the report were wrong, too.

But even if all the information is correct, a report is not just a list of facts. Your facts have to be put in order so they make sense. A report on how pioneers made soap is hard to understand if the last steps in soap making are explained before the first steps.

Don't confuse your reader! In a report on lizards, for instance, the facts about where they live should all be together. The facts about what they eat should go in another section or paragraph. An unorganized jumble of information is no fun to read.

Doing a report involves a lot more than writing the sentences and paragraphs. You'll spend as much time gathering information and organizing it in a logical way as you will writing the actual report. And the better you do each of these steps, the better your report will be in the end.

MAKE YOUR REPORT YOUR OWN

What makes your report different from someone else's? If teachers assign the same topic to everyone in the class, why don't they get thirty reports that are exactly alike? Because no matter what the topic is, each person thinks about it in his or her own way. Suppose your teacher asks for a report on snow rescue teams. You might wonder what kind of clothes the teams wear on their rescue missions. But your friend wants to know how cold it gets in the mountains.

Both of your reports will include some facts about clothing and weather. But your report won't sound exactly the same as your friend's. The parts of a topic you think are the most interesting are the ones you will write the most about. Your view of a topic and your selection of facts makes the report you write your very own—different from everyone else's.

YOUR REPORT

In early winter, it is not very cold in the mountains. The rescue teams wear warm boots and down jackets. They have goggles to keep the sun out of their eyes.

Later it gets really cold. The teams wear ski masks and down hoods. They wear two pairs of mittens. They have thermal socks and special boots. They have to be careful so their fingers and toes don't get frostbite. Sometimes doctors have to cut off frostbitten toes.

YOUR FRIEND'S REPORT

Snow rescue teams work outdoors all winter in the mountains. The rescue teams wear special clothes to keep them warm.

In November and December, the daytime temperature is about 25 degrees Fahrenheit. At night it drops as low as 0 degrees.

In January and February, it gets really cold. It can be lower than 0 degrees Fahrenheit during the day. The lowest temperature it ever got was 52 degrees below 0. Even when it's this cold, rescue teams keep on working.

These two reports are on the same topic—snow rescue teams. But the two writers were interested in different details about the teams' work. Each report has a different point of view on the subject. And each gives the reader a new look at the same topic.

This difference is what makes your report yours. When your teacher reads thirty reports on the same topic, none of them will be exactly alike.

CHAPTER 2

CHOOSING A TOPIC

HOW DO YOU DECIDE WHAT TO write a report on? First, it should be something you are interested in. You'll do a better job and have more fun if you pick a topic you'd like to learn more about.

But what if your teacher tells the whole class to write about the same thing? This often happens in social studies and science classes. Even then, you can make some choices of your own. Almost any topic is too big for a short report.

What if the report topic is dinosaurs? Each person can write about one part of this topic. There's lots of dinosaur lore that is fun to explore. Maybe you'd like to know more about where dinosaur bones have been found. Or you might want to find out why dinosaurs became extinct. Types of dinosaurs and what they looked like could be a report topic. Or perhaps you'd like to discuss the information scientists have uncovered about the size of dinosaur eggs.

You can't possibly cover the whole topic of dinosaurs. There is just too much information to be crammed into a school report. Your first job is to choose a part of the topic that is small enough to explain in just a few pages.

The whole idea of writing a report is to give some detailed information about a topic. Details make your report interesting to read. Suppose the topic is earthquakes. You might decide to write about major earthquakes all over the world. But when you began your research, you would soon discover that there have been far too many to write about in one report. Even if you narrowed your topic to include only U.S. earthquakes, you wouldn't have room to do much more than make a list of them. A list like this, even if you wrote it in sentences, would not make a very good report.

But how about writing on the three biggest U.S. earthquakes since 1900? Then you could tell more than just the dates and places where they happened. In your report, you could compare the force of the three earthquakes and the amount of damage they caused. Or you might want to report on only one of the three biggest earthquakes. If you write about just the most recent serious earthquake in California, you will be able to add many more details. You can tell how many aftershocks there were and how long it took to repair the damage. You might even have room to tell a little about how people's daily lives were changed by the earthquake.

Writing about a smaller portion of a large topic means that you can use more details. This makes a better report. But be careful not to make your topic *too* small. Then you might not be able to find any information about it. For example, your teacher might tell everyone to write a report on Korea. You must choose which part or aspect of this topic you'd like to write about. You might decide to do your report on the games children play in Korea. But what if you can find very little information on this topic? Unless you know someone who lived in Korea and can tell you about the games kids play there, it might be better to look for another topic.

If you run into this problem, keep making your topic slightly bigger until you've got something you *can* find out about. For instance, the report on games children play in Korea can be broadened to include other parts of a Korean child's life. You will probably be able to find some information about schools and families, even if you can't find out much on games. Once you think of a topic for your report, it is a good idea to talk to your teacher about it. He or she may know how much information is available for you to use.

Whatever topic you choose, make sure it isn't boring to you. Writing a report takes time and lots of work. You won't do your best job if you start out with a topic you don't like.

CHAPTER 3

FINDING FACTS

NOW THAT YOU HAVE CHOSEN your topic, you need to gather the information you will put in your report. Digging out the facts is called doing research. A lot of people really enjoy searching for information on a topic. And it's a very important step. If you don't do any research, you won't have anything to write in your report.

Start as early as you can. It may take awhile to find all the sources of information you need to look at. And when you've found them, you'll need time to read all those facts. Besides, when you've finished doing your research, you'll still have the report to write.

Where can you look for information

about your topic? Often the easiest and most useful way is to start with a general reference source, such as an encyclopedia. You've probably used an encyclopedia before. It's a set of books that has articles on most subjects that people want to know about. Almost every library has several different encyclopedias. You can also use encyclopedias on a computer.

Encyclopedia articles are in alphabetical order. They tell the basic facts about each subject. Encyclopedia articles give some details, but of course they don't have as much information as a whole book on the topic. The last volume is the index to all the other volumes; it will tell you where to find articles on your topic.

An encyclopedia article on a big topic may be quite long. Look at the headings to find the paragraphs that cover what you want to know. At the end of some articles, you may find titles of other articles that tell more about your topic.

Many encyclopedias and other reference works on a computer are actually books that have been copied onto software so you can read the information on the screen. You'll need to follow the online directions to get the article you want.

It's always a good idea to find out when any reference work you are using was published. This tells you how up-to-date the information is. But how can you find out when something was published? Look for the copyright date—a year with the word "copyright" and/or the symbol ©, like this:

Copyright © 2000

In a book, the copyright date is usually on a page near the front. Online, look at the bottom of the first screen for the copyright information.

The reason you want the latest information for your report is that things change. What if new facts have been learned about an old discovery or invention? And if your report is on something that keeps happening, like earthquakes or floods, you'll want to make sure you've got the most recent information.

What other reference sources can you use? An atlas is a collection of maps, but it also has lots of other information. It lists the populations of countries and big cities. It may give facts about climate, time zones, crops, and many other topics. If you're doing a report on weather systems around the world or the principal resources of your state, an atlas may have much of the information you need. For any report that deals with physical information about the United States or the world, an atlas is a good place to check for information.

Another helpful reference book is a yearly almanac. Almanacs are fat books that are filled with odd and unusual facts. Almanacs are sometimes available on computer, but they're usually more fun to flip through in book form.

An almanac may contain a brief history of the United States and of the world, sports statistics, information about pets, descriptions of all the national parks, and lots more. When you have some spare time, you might want to glance through an almanac; you'll be amazed at all the strange things you can find out.

As you do your research, you may come across words you don't understand. A dictionary will tell you what they mean and how to pronounce them. Dictionaries, too, are sometimes online, but it's handy to have one in book form so it's always available. Many of the larger ("unabridged") dictionaries also have color pictures of things like state flags, birds, and precious stones.

Reading what the reference sources have to say about your topic isn't the end of your search for information. Now you're ready to read something that gives some additional details. But how can you find more on your topic?

CHAPTER 4

SEARCHING THE LIBRARY

NOW THAT YOU HAVE AN OVERVIEW of your topic, you will probably want to read something with more details. One good place to look is in the library. As you know, libraries are full of books! And these books cover a vast number of topics. But how can you find what you want on all those shelves and shelves of volumes?

All libraries are set up pretty much the same way. The books are divided into fiction and nonfiction. Fiction books have stories in them; nonfiction books have facts.

Fiction is arranged in alphabetical order according to the author's last name. The shelves that hold the fiction books usually have letters on them, such as "A–B," so you know where to start looking for the book you want.

Nonfiction is arranged differently. There are so many nonfiction books on different subjects in a library that they have to be arranged by topic. If they were put in order alphabetically by author, books on each topic would be scattered all over the library. If you wanted a book on the solar system, you would have no idea where to look. Putting all the books on one topic together makes it easy to find information about that topic.

Each nonfiction book in the library has a label with a number on it. The number tells what topic the book is about. This method of using numbers to organize nonfiction books was invented by Melvil Dewey; it's called the Dewey decimal classification system.

All the books with the same number are gathered together on the same library shelf. The shelves of nonfiction books usually have numbers on them, such as "500–599," so you know where to start looking for the books you want. For example, all the books in the 500s are about science. All the

551.2 books are about the smaller topic of earthquakes. If you wanted to locate a book about earthquakes, you would look for books labeled with the number 551.2.

But how do you know what number your topic has? You don't have to walk past all the shelves, hoping you'll spot it by accident! There is an easier way. You can look up your report topic in the library catalog.

Libraries have their catalogs on computer, so it's simple to find what you're looking for. Although each system may be slightly different, the way they are set up is the same. You can look books up by title, author name, or subject. (To operate your library's computer catalog, read the directions on the computer terminal or ask a librarian for help.)

If you know the title of a book you want, you can do a title search on the library computer. If you know the author's name, you can type the author's last name onto the screen and start looking that way. But if you don't have any specific books in mind, you'll want to look up your topic on the subject screen and see what books are available. No matter how you look up the book you want—

whether by title, author, or subject—you'll still need to use the library computer catalog first. That's because without the Dewey decimal number (sometimes called the "call number"), you won't know where to find your book on the shelves.

For instance, what if your topic is earthquakes and someone told you about a great book on the subject? To find the book, you'd still have to look it up to get its number. Once you have the number, you can find the shelves where that book and others on the same topic are located.

Here's what one library's computer catalog screen said about a book on earthquakes:

```
AUTHOR:     Branley, Franklyn M.
TITLE:      Earthquakes / by Franklyn M. Branley ;
            illustrated by Richard Rosenblum.
PUBLISHER:  New York : Crowell, c1990
DESCRIPT:   32 p. : col. ill. ; 19 x 24 cm.
SERIES:     A Let's-read-and-find-out science book
SUMMARY:    Discusses why earthquakes happen, what
            their sometimes devastating effects are,
            where the danger zones are, and what
            measures people can take to safeguard
            themselves.
LOCATION:   JUV 551.22 B
```

You can see that the title line gives the title of the book, the author's name, and the illustrator's name. The publisher line tells where the publishing house is located, the name of the publisher, and the book's copyright date.

The "Descript" (description) for this book tells how many pages the book has and that it has color illustrations; it also gives the dimensions of the book in centimeters.

You might wonder why anyone would care how many pages a book has or what size those pages are. You may even think it's dumb to have someone enter all this information for every book in the library, but it's not. First of all, this description gives you an idea of what the book you want looks like, if it's fat or skinny. When you go to the shelf where the book is kept, you'll know about how big the book is and it will be easier to spot.

Another reason this information is helpful is that it tells you how long the book is. If you've got a report to write in the next few days, you don't want to start reading a two-hundred-page book about the subject now!

Reading the summary lets you know what's in the book. This will give you a clue about how useful this book might be.

Probably the most important information on

this catalog screen is the location of the book. This book's call number (or Dewey decimal number) is JUV (for Juvenile) 551.22 B. Now all you need to do is look for shelves in the children's section with the 551 numbers, and you're all set.

But what if you don't have a specific book in mind and you're not even sure what to call the topic? If your report is on poodles, do you look up "poodles" or "dogs"? The only way to find out is to try. Always begin with the most specific topic name you can think of. In this case, you would first type in "poodle" on the subject screen. If something comes up, you're ready to go searching for books. But there may be no listing under "poodle." Then you can try the larger heading "dogs." Sometimes books are listed under rather strange-sounding topics, so if you can't find what you want, ask the librarian.

Many library computer catalogs have other information about the books. In some libraries, you can see on the screen whether a book is available (not checked out) and even the titles of books near it on the shelf. But don't pin your hopes on only one book that appears to be what you want and also seems to be available in this library. Computer catalog information is not always up-to-the-minute. The only way you can find out for sure what's available is to go to the shelves and look at the books themselves.

Once you've found out where at least one book on your topic is located, go to that section and take a look at what's there. The titles of the books make a good starting place. As you read along the shelf, you will see a number of titles that don't sound very helpful. For example, if your topic is dinosaur fossils, a book entitled *Dinosaurs of North America* might be useful, but the information will be limited to North America. Still, you'll probably find several books that look as though they might help you with your report. Take them over to a table and look inside. How can you decide which books cover your topic best?

At the beginning of many nonfiction books is a table of contents, which lists the chapter titles and the page numbers the chapters begin on. Read through the chapter titles. Do any of them seem to be just what you're looking for? If so, this is a book to check out. For example, your report might be on endangered sea animals. In a book entitled *The Sea Otter,* the chapters "From the Brink of Extinction" and "Otter Rescue" will probably have information you want.

A book's index also tells you what information the book contains. An index is found on the last pages of many nonfiction books. It is an alphabetical listing of names and ideas contained in the book, with the page numbers where you can find them. The index of *The Sea Otter* tells you that the Endangered Species Act is discussed on page 49 and extinction is mentioned on pages 7, 8, and 33.

INDEX

Sometimes it isn't clear from a table of contents whether your topic is included in that book. At these times, an index is especially helpful, because it lists everything the book talks about.

Checking a book's table of contents and index saves time. You don't have to read the whole book to find out whether it has the facts you need. This is a good way to choose the books you'll use for your research.

Here's another way to speed your research along. Does the book you're looking at have a bibliography or a list of further reading? A bibliography is a list of books the author used in doing research for this book. A list of further reading gives the names of other books an author thinks readers would find interesting or useful. You'll get some good clues that will lead you to other resources. Isn't it nice when someone else has done some of the work for you?

FURTHER READING

Bailey, Jane H. *The Sea Otter's Struggle*. Chicago: Follett, 1973.

Bailey Jill. *Otter Rescue*. Austin, TX: Steck-Vaughn, 1992.

Chanin, Paul. *The Natural History of Otters*. New York: Facts On File, 1985.

Holyer, Ernie M. *The Southern Sea Otter*. Austin, TX: Steck-Vaughn, 1975.

León, Vicki. *A Raft of Sea Otters: An Affectionate Portrait*. San Luis Obispo, CA: Blake Publishing, 1987.

Paine, Stefani. *The World of the Sea Otter*. San Francisco: Sierra Club Books, 1993.

Smith, Roland. *Sea Otter Rescue: The Aftermath of an Oil Spill*. New York: Dutton, 1990.

Friends of the Sea Otter publishes magazines, *The Otter Raft* and *Otter Pup*.

CHAPTER 5

SEARCHING THE INTERNET

IT'S TOO BAD THE INTERNET ISN'T organized logically, the way a library is. But it's not, and the online sites outnumber the books in even a large library. On the Internet, anyone can get information and ideas from all over the world. No one owns the Internet, and no one is really in charge. This can create a lot of confusion.

One way people have tried to deal with the confusion is by making directories of Internet sites according to their subjects. These directories are often called "Internet search engines"; Yahoo and Excite! are a couple of examples.

Directory makers try to keep up-to-date. They list new sites and make sure the addresses of old sites are still correct. If you click on a search engine, or directory, you'll get instructions on how to find out what's available on a topic. But remember that Internet sites come online and disappear or change addresses often; this makes it hard to keep up. So if you can't find what you're looking for with one search engine, try another to see if it has a listing that looks useful.

Another method of finding information about your topic is to use the "favorite links" lists that are on many Web sites. These links usually connect to other Internet sites on the same or similar topics. So if you find one Web site that isn't quite what you want but is on the right topic, why not check out its links? One of them may take you to an Internet site that's perfect for your report.

Looking at a site's address carefully will help you in your Internet search. The three extension letters after the dot in the main part of the address tell you what kind of site it is. For instance, <.gov> means a government site, while <.com> means a commercial site (one run by a company). Countries have their own two-letter extensions as well. If you see <.ca>, it means Canada, not California.

The extension <.edu> means it's an educational site. If the site is a college or university main page, you'll probably find lots of helpful information. But remember that students and teachers at that college can usually put up personal pages with the <.edu> extension, and these may not be as reliable.

The number of three-letter extensions used for site categories keeps growing, so try to be alert to these changes. This is one way the Internet community is trying to get the Net organized!

As you search the Web, you'll become more familiar with the various parts of site addresses and what they mean. The more information you can get from a site address, the easier your Internet search will become. Before long you'll be breezing through FAQs (Frequently Asked Questions), jumping from link to link, and wondering why your class hasn't put up its own Web page about writing reports yet!

Another way to deal with the Internet confusion is to use a private online service, such as America Online. Private online services cost money, usually a monthly fee. These services control what kinds of sites are on their system, and they can organize the information into channels so it's easier to find what you want. If you've got a private online service account for your computer at home or at school, you might want to use this before attempting to search the entire Internet.

CHAPTER 6

FINDING MORE INFORMATION

YOU CAN DO RESEARCH IN LOTS OF places that you might not have thought about. Here are some ideas to get you started.

A museum may be just the place to gather information for your report. Many cities have several museums. If you don't know much about the museums where you live, check the yellow pages for the addresses and phone numbers. When you call, you may get a recorded message that tells you when the museum is open and what kinds of things are in it. Some museums charge admission fees—be sure to listen for this. If you talk to a live person, ask whether there is a discount for children your age.

Many museums have Web sites, and more are going online all the time. Some of these sites are very elaborate and can take you on a virtual tour of some or all of the exhibits. While you probably can't drop in this afternoon at a museum on the other side of the world, you may be able to visit it in cyberspace. One of the main attractions of these online museum sites is the chance to look at special exhibits that you may never see in person. But to get a feel for the size of museum pieces and the vibrancy of their colors and textures, it's best to see them in real life.

A museum of natural history usually has exhibits about animals, plants, fish, and rocks. In fact, anything that has to do with the earth and its living creatures might be on exhibit. If you are doing a report on a topic like dinosaurs or giant redwoods or undersea exploration, a natural history museum could be a good place to look for information.

Art museums often have other things besides paintings and sculpture. For example, tapestries, jewelry, or pottery might be exhibited. For a report on Egypt, take a look at the Egyptian pieces in an art museum. Seeing a real mummy case might give you a terrific new idea for your report.

Museum gift shops often have pictures of their exhibits on inexpensive postcards. Maybe you'll find one that's perfect for your report's cover.

Local city or county museums often deal with the history of where you live. They have hand-crafted items that were made nearby, exhibits about the environment of your area, and information about the people who first lived there. If you are doing a report on something that happened near your town, the local museum may have information about it.

Lots of special museums are scattered all over the country. Depending on where you live, you could be close to a museum of trains, ships, antique cars, stamps, ocean fish, comics, or almost anything else you can think of. These museums may be quite small, but the people who work in them are usually happy to help you find what you need.

Do you like to watch TV? Often you can find out facts for a report by watching a TV show. A program on penguins will give you lots of tips for a report on Antarctica. News specials during presidential election campaigns are a good source of information about how our system of government works. Televised international sports competitions, such as the Olympics and world championship skiing, swimming, or soccer, often include interviews with young athletes about their training and home life. If you have cable TV, you can find channels that specialize in history, science, the arts, and other topics. And of course, lots of PBS shows are packed with facts you can use in reports.

Don't forget newspapers and magazines as sources for topic information. There are lots of specialty magazines, and one of them might have information for you. In addition to tons of facts, well-known magazines like *National Geographic* have wonderful maps and color photos that you could copy for your report.

The daily newspaper often has informative articles on current events, along with charts and graphs. Graphics like these can help both you and your report's reader get a better grasp of your topic.

Historical locations are hard to visit in person unless you happen to live near one. But many online sites focus on historical events and locations. Government sites, for instance, may provide lots of factual information, as well as photos, about places like Mount Rushmore. And city or national park sites often can give you a feeling of almost having been there.

Think about your topic. Is there someone you can talk to who can give you firsthand information? In addition to reading about being a veterinarian or how to take care of a sick puppy, why not interview a vet in your town and find out what he or she has to say? If your topic is safety in the home, talking to a firefighter, police officer, and Red Cross first-aid instructor will probably give you enough information for a whole report.

Don't forget e-mail as a way to talk to people. Many sites have e-mail addresses where you can send your questions. Often experts are more than willing to offer their opinions or suggest other places for you to check out. For instance, university Web sites sometimes list e-mail addresses for professors in various fields, so you can write to them.

You may think that college professors have better things to do than answer your e-mail, but think again! Most professors are totally fascinated by what they teach. And they may be so impressed that a kid like you is really interested that they'll spend quite a bit of time coming up with answers. Just be sure to ask questions you can't easily get answers to in other places. For instance, a professor of geology won't be pleased if you ask her to tell you what a volcano is—you could find that information in an encyclopedia. But she may be delighted to e-mail you her opinion on whether Mount Saint Helens will erupt again anytime soon.

Have you heard your grandfather talk about how he first came to the United States as a boy? Maybe the lady next door likes to tell you what your town was like long before you were born. When you listen to these people, you are hearing oral history. This is history that is told, not written down. The facts and details these people remember often are not in any books. And you can ask whatever questions you like. A book doesn't answer you the way a real live person does. Listening to oral history makes the past come alive. You will feel as though you were there yourself.

Everyone you talk to knows a lot about something. But the person who has special information for your report could be *you*. If your teacher assigns national parks as a topic, why not write about one you've been to? You'll need to get some facts from reference books or online. But nothing you read can tell you what it feels like to hike down the Bright Angel Trail in the Grand Canyon, get sprayed by a geyser at Yellowstone, or touch Spanish moss hanging from the trees in the Everglades. Including your own memories or experiences in your report can make it extra exciting.

Pretend you're a detective. As you search for information on your topic, imagine other places you might look. People are usually glad to help you. Don't be afraid to explore. You might uncover a gold mine!

CHAPTER 7

WHAT "FACTS" ARE REALLY TRUE?

As YOU SEARCH FOR INFORMATION on your topic, you may run into "facts" that don't agree. For instance, what if your report is on Pocahontas? Maybe one source gives her birth date as 1595; another lists it as 1598; and a third says no one is sure exactly what year she was born. How do you know what's correct?

This is a time to use your own good judgment and common sense. If none of the three sources gives any reason for listing one birth date instead of another, you can say that Pocahontas was born in the 1590s but that sources disagree on the exact year.

But sometimes new information comes to light. What if one of your sources says that a diary written in 1595 has been discovered? And what if the writer of the diary tells about visiting Chief Powhatan and his newborn daughter Pocahontas? Then you can feel pretty certain of this famous woman's birth date—at least until someone discovers new, and different, information!

The dates given for events that happened long ago may change with each new piece of information. These events may have occurred before written records were common, so it may be hard to find out the facts. Often the search for new information about these very old dates can go on for a very long time.

Here's a good general rule to follow about conflicting facts: If two sources disagree, look for a third source and see if there is a majority opinion. Also check to find out when these conflicting sources were written. New discoveries are made all the time, and people come up with new ways of looking at existing facts. So a more recent source is likely to have the latest information.

But there's another important question: Are your sources all reliable? This is not always the case. You need to think about where your information comes from.

Books published by well-known companies tend to have reliable information. These books are checked for accuracy several times before they are sold to the public. When a mistake does slip through, publishers try to correct it. If the mistake is an important one, such as a misprint that could be dangerous in a recipe, the publisher will take back all the books and replace them with new, corrected ones.

Well-known magazines and newspapers are also usually published by large companies whose reputations depend on the accuracy and reliability of what they sell. Because magazines, and especially newspapers, are published every month or week or even every day, the facts they contain can't be checked as carefully as the information in books. But when there is a mistake, newspapers and magazines can publish a correction quickly.

Factual television shows are also created by large companies that care about their reputations. Television documentaries are expensive to make, so these companies want to be sure they get things right. Reviewers are quick to point out errors, and people who work on poorly researched programs may not keep their jobs for long.

Did you know that many writers of television

documentaries use children's nonfiction books as the basis of their research? It's true! Children's nonfiction books have a reputation for being accurate, well researched, and clearly written.

Companies that make other types of informational products, like CD-ROMs, also hire careful researchers. They look for writers who are known for accurate work.

What about information on the Internet? Some of it is as reliable as books and television documentaries. If what you're looking at are actual pages of a book, such as an online encyclopedia, then the information you read is as accurate as the book itself. It's simply online for your convenience.

But much of the information on the Internet is not checked for accuracy by anyone except the person who wrote it. Pages created for the Internet are often written by people who don't know much about the topic. Even large companies often have no regular employee who's in charge of their Web pages. Still, if you find inaccurate or misleading information on a big company's Web site, you can write to the company and they will probably try to fix it.

However, the Internet is crowded with Web pages created by all sorts of people, and these people may or may not be experts on their topics. Even when the writers are trying to be accurate and careful, they often make mistakes. And there's no one checking their work to make sure it's correct.

Even worse, some people put information on the Internet that they know is inaccurate or misleading. Why do they do this? It's hard to know. But there is no way right now to prevent it. On the Internet, people can say whatever they want to. So long as what they say doesn't actually break the law, their Web sites will remain online.

Often it's hard to tell who puts up a particular Web site. This is both good and bad. It's good because people can provide information without fear of being put in jail. In countries where the government keeps information from getting to the people, this offers a way to exchange ideas freely.

But it can be bad, because anyone can put anything online without caring whether it's true. When you put up a Web site, you don't have to tell who you really are or where you're really located. So it may be very difficult to find out who is spreading false information.

What this means is that you have to consider the reliability of your sources of information carefully. When reading anything—especially something online—ask yourself, Who wrote this? What does this person know about the subject? Where did he or she get this information? Might he or she have a reason to distort the facts on this subject?

Also remember that there's a difference between facts and opinions or theories. A fact is a piece of information that most people accept as true. Scientists and others are always trying to learn whether facts are true—but sometimes this takes a long time. For example, people used to "know" that the earth was flat; that was considered a fact back then. But eventually explorers were able to discover that the earth is round.

There are probably many "facts" that are accepted today but will be proved incorrect in the future. Discoveries, both great and small, are made all the time. But until a fact has been convincingly disproved, it remains as close to the truth as we can get.

Opinions and interpretations are the conclusions people come to when they've considered the facts. Intelligent people may often disagree about how to interpret a certain set of facts. When you write a report, you give your own interpretation of the facts you have learned. Just make sure you start with facts that are as true as possible.

CHAPTER 8

WHAT DO YOU WANT TO KNOW?

SOMETIMES IT SEEMS AS IF THERE are *too* many places to look for information. It's hard to figure out where to start. Before you run off to the library or log onto the Internet or ask someone for an interview, think about your topic. The reason you chose this topic is that you would like to know more about it. What exactly do you want to know?

If the topic is dinosaurs and you've read that some scientists now think they may have been warm-blooded, you might do your report on warm-blooded dinosaurs. What questions could you ask to get the information you want? First, did warm-blooded dinosaurs really exist? What does "warm-blooded" mean, anyway? What makes scientists think dinosaurs were warm-blooded? How can these scientists prove they are right? The answers to these questions are the information you need to write your report.

How will you keep track of all this information? You need to take notes. There are lots of different ways of taking notes. Some people use index cards; some use notebook paper; some scribble on little scraps of paper and then lose them in the laundry! But one easy way to keep track of your notes is to make a large chart.

You could create a chart on a computer, but for note taking it's easiest just to use a big piece of paper. You can cut open a paper shopping bag so it lies flat or tape several sheets of plain typing paper together. In fact, any kind of paper that's big enough is fine.

Divide the paper into columns—you'll need one column for each question you want to answer, plus a column to list the books you use. A ruler or yardstick will help you keep the lines neat and clear. Make the boxes large enough for two or three sentences. Write one of your questions at the top of each column.

In the first column, write down the name of each book you are using (you can shorten it if you want) and the name of its author. Also write down the year the book was published. This information is found on the copyright page of the book. For example, if you look at the copyright page of this book, you will see that it was first published in 1983 and was updated in 1998. (You can use the copyright date as the date of publication. In most cases, they are the same.)

If you are interviewing someone, write down his or her name and phone number and the date of the interview in the first column. For a source on the Internet, write down the Internet address and any other information that is provided, including the date the item was posted or updated.

Now stop for a moment. Does your teacher want you to include a bibliography or a list of sources at the end of your report? If so, now is the time to write down all the information you'll need. A bibliography should list:

- the author of the book, article, or Internet site
- the title of the book, article, or Internet site
- the name and location (city and state) of

the book or magazine publisher, or the address of the Internet site
- the date the book or article was published or the Internet site was last updated
- the name of any person you interview and the date of the interview

If your teacher wants you to list the page numbers where you found information for your report, be sure to note these down on your list.

Now you are ready to start taking notes. In your first research book, find the paragraphs or sections that talk about your topic. As you read, keep your questions in mind. Look for information that answers your questions. Write it down in the correct box.

Do the same for each book or article you read and each person you interview. When your chart is filled, you will be able to see at a glance what information you have about each of your questions. You'll fill in the "conclusions" boxes later (see Chapter 10).

	Did warm-blooded dinos exist?	What does warm-blooded mean?	What makes scientists now think some dinos were warm-blooded?	What evidence are scientists looking for?
Young Oxford Book of the Prehistoric World, Bailey & Seddon, 1995				
Dinosaur Worlds, Don Lessem, 1996				
Compton's Encyclopedia, 1994				
Internet: *Scientific American*, 1997				
Conclusions				

CHAPTER 9

TAKING NOTES

NOTES ARE REMINDERS OF WHAT you've read or heard. They keep you from getting mixed up about who said what. You won't forget an important fact if it's in your notes.

You can write your notes either as whole sentences or as short phrases. Just make sure that your notes are not as long as the book you are reading! You should be able to sum up the main idea of a paragraph in one or two sentences. Suppose you read this paragraph:

The bones of the plant-eating dinosaur *Massospondylus* show growth rings, like those of a cold-blooded animal. But the bones of some dinosaurs show no rings of growth when viewed in cross section. The bones of warm-blooded animals show no growth rings. (*Dinosaur Worlds,* p. 55)

Your notes might say something like this:

Some dino bones have growth rings, which means c-b; but others don't, so maybe w-b.

You can use abbreviations of long words to save space. You might write "dino" for "dinosaur." And "w-b" and "c-b" could stand for "warm-blooded" and "cold-blooded." It's best to abbreviate only the words that are used often in your notes. That way you'll be sure to remember what each abbreviation stands for.

Remember that you are reading to find out answers to the questions at the top of your chart. You don't have to sum up everything the book's author says. Take notes only on the information that helps answer your questions.

Your notes should be written in your own words, not copied from the book. After you've read

	Did warm-blooded dinos exist?	What does warm-blooded mean?	What makes scientists now think some dinos were warm-blooded?	What evidence are scientists looking for?
Young Oxford Book of the Prehistoric World, Bailey & Seddon, 1995				
Dinosaur Worlds, Don Lessem, 1996			Some dino bones have growth rings, which means c-b; but others don't, so maybe w-b.	
Compton's Encyclopedia, 1994				
Internet: *Scientific American*, 1997				
Conclusions				

a paragraph or short section of information on your topic, mark your place with a slip of paper and close the book. Now write down the main idea in your own words. If you're reading information on the computer, darken the screen while you make your notes. Or if you printed the information from the computer, turn the paper over while you write notes in your own words.

Why is it so important not to use the exact words from the book or the computer in your notes? There are two reasons. First, this is a way of making sure you understand what you have read. It's pretty hard to write a report if you don't really understand the information you've collected. But you know you've got the idea when you can explain it in your own way.

The other reason is that your report should be your own work. Copying from a book or from several books is not the same as writing a report. It may seem easier to write down the exact words from a book or from the computer on your note chart. But you will use the words in your notes when you sit down to write your report. And you won't remember then that these are another author's words, not your own. When your notes are in your own words, you can use these sentences in your report.

Of course, changing the words doesn't mean that you change the facts. If you read that some dinosaur fossils were found in the Zambezi River Valley in Africa, you can't say they were found in Iceland. That would be making up a new "fact," and it wouldn't be true.

Facts belong to everybody. The location of a dinosaur fossil is a fact that anyone can read about and use. Putting the facts you learn in your report is not stealing. But you cannot write them in exactly the same way another author has. You can't pretend that someone else's sentences are your own. If you do use sentences from a book, you must put quotation marks around them and tell your reader where you read them.

As you take notes, remember that library books do not belong to you. When you close the book to write down a main idea in your notes, use a slip of paper to mark your place. Don't bend down the corner of the page. And never write anything in a library book. There's nothing more annoying than trying to read a book that someone else has marked up.

You also need to take notes when you talk to someone to get information for your report. Use the same kind of chart, and write down the answers to your questions as you listen.

Most people are happy to share their knowledge. But since you'll be taking up their time, try to get organized beforehand. When you make an appointment to talk to someone, be on time. Bring your own pencil and chart for notes. And be prepared with your questions. Also, don't forget to say thank you at the end of the interview. It never hurts to be polite. Besides, you might need to go back for a second interview!

CHAPTER 10

GETTING READY TO WRITE

ONCE YOU HAVE WRITTEN ALL your notes on your chart, you are ready to organize your information. What conclusions can you come to?

Look at all the notes in the first column, which are the answers to your first question. Do they all say more or less the same thing? If so, write a sentence that sums up the main idea in the "conclusions" box at the bottom of that column. Do the same for each column in your chart.

This can be tricky. You may have found different answers to your questions in the research materials you used. When authors don't agree, you have to see if you can figure out why.

There are many reasons why authors disagree about a topic. New information may have been discovered recently, but a book that was published before this new discovery won't mention it. Even a recent book won't have this information if the author didn't hear about it. For example, scientists used to think that dinosaurs that walked on their two hind legs, such as *Tyrannosaurus rex,* dragged their tails on the ground behind them. But then they discovered new evidence. It showed that these dinosaurs kept their tails lifted above the ground for balance. Books that were published before this discovery have pictures of *Tyrannosaurus rex* with its tail in the wrong position.

Sometimes scientists come up with a new idea or theory about how something happened. Until they prove that the theory is true, some people will believe it and some won't. This means that books on this topic may disagree.

There are other times when you might find different answers to one of your questions. For instance, maybe one book on dog care says puppies that are less than four months old have to be paper trained. But when you interview a woman who runs dog training classes, she says that puppies should be trained to go to the bathroom outdoors as soon as they are old enough to leave their mothers.

The author of the dog care book and the woman who teaches the classes both know a lot about dogs. Maybe both of them are right. They disagree on the best way to train a puppy, but they agree that puppies can be trained in some way.

When you find disagreement between the answers to one of your questions, you may need two sentences for the "conclusions" box of that column. Your "conclusions" sentences for this question might be:

Puppies can be trained to go to the bathroom outdoors. They can also be paper trained.

There won't be any disagreement in your notes on some topics. But if there is, try to figure out what the disagreement means. Perhaps both books are partly right. Or maybe you can think of a reason why one book is wrong. What you say about this disagreement is part of what makes the report your own, not just a copy of the books you've read.

When the "conclusions" boxes at the bottom of your chart are filled in, you are ready to decide how your report will be organized. In some ways, writing a report is like telling a story. Your report will have a beginning, a middle, and an end.

For some topics, deciding what comes first is easy. If your report tells how to make chocolate chip cookies, the first information the reader needs is the list of ingredients. Next you explain, in the right order, the steps for mixing up the ingredients. Then you tell how to put the dough on the cookie sheet and how long and at what temperature to bake the cookies. Last you could tell how good they taste when they're done. Whenever you are telling how to do something—housebreak a puppy, build a model, or learn to be a lifeguard—you will quickly see that there is a natural order to follow.

The order in which you write about other kinds of topics may be harder to figure out. Look at the note chart about warm-blooded dinosaurs on pages 62–63. This report could be organized in a couple of different ways. You might decide that the first part of your report should answer the question "Did warm-blooded dinosaurs exist?" Then you could explain what "warm-blooded" means. Next you might tell why scientists began to think that some dinosaurs were warm-blooded instead of cold-blooded. And finally you could describe what evidence scientists are looking for in order to prove their theory. This is the same order as the questions at the top of the notes chart.

But there is another way to organize this report. You could start out by defining what "warm-blooded" means. Next you could describe why some scientists now think that some dinosaurs were warm-blooded, and then tell what other evidence they hope to find. At the end of your report, you could explain why the question "Did warm-blooded dinosaurs exist?" can't be answered for sure.

Either way you decided to organize this report on warm-blooded dinosaurs would make sense to the reader. The important point to keep in mind is that you are the person who has the information. You are trying to pass it on to your reader. Think of what things the reader needs to know first. Pretend you are explaining your topic to a friend who doesn't know anything about it. What would you have to say first so your friend could understand the rest of your explanation?

The sentences in the "conclusions" boxes of

	Did warm-blooded dinos exist?	What does warm-blooded mean?	What makes scientists now think some dinos were warm-blooded?	What evidence are scientists looking for?
Young Oxford Book of the Prehistoric World, Bailey & Seddon, 1995	Some sci's think so, but no one knows for sure.		Evidence for w-b: some dinos' legs were directly under body (like mammals & birds); some had large blood vessels in legs (like mammals).	Study fossil nests to find out how fast dinos grew; w-b animals grow faster than c-b ones.
Dinosaur Worlds, Don Lessem, 1996	Some were c-b, but maybe some were w-b.		Some dino bones have growth rings, which means c-b; but others don't, so maybe w-b.	Study growth rings in bones to see if same as c-b animals today.
Compton's Encyclopedia, 1994	Not yet known, but maybe neither c-b nor w-b.	W-b animals can maintain body temp & be very active. C-b animals' body temp is same as air or water around them; can't be active for long.	Many dinos walked upright and ran, not crawled, so maybe w-b. But if w-b, huge bodies would overheat. Some sci's think huge dinos were "gigantothermic" (warm up slowly in sun, cool down slowly at night), more like c-b than w-b.	

Internet: *Scientific American*, 1997	Not proved yet.		Some small dinos had big brains, which maybe means w-b. Fossil tracks show some dinos were very social, which maybe means w-b. Dino fossils don't have bones in nose that keep w-b animals from drying out; but maybe didn't need them if climate was wetter.	Study bones to see if growth rings show how fast dinos grew; if so, rings don't indicate c-b or w-b. Search for nose structures. Look for more evidence about social behavior of dinos.
Conclusions	Some sci's think some dinos were w-b, but not proved yet.	W-b means body is always the same temp.	Much evidence shows that some were w-b, but many things not known yet.	Different kinds of new evidence may help answer questions.

each column of your chart are the main ideas for each paragraph or section of your report. Once you have figured out what order you think your information should be written in, list these main ideas in that order. Be sure to leave some space between them. Then you can put whatever details you have under each main idea. This list is an outline. It will be a kind of map for you to follow when you write your report.

Most reports need an ending paragraph. This can be a summary of what you've said in your report. Another way to end is to tell why your topic is an interesting one. Whatever way you decide to end your report, be sure to add a sentence to the end of your outline so you will remember what you planned to say.

You may wonder whether all this work is necessary. Wouldn't it be easier just to start writing and hope for the best? The answer is no. When you think about your topic and the questions you plan to answer in your report, you get a clear idea in your mind of what you want to say. This makes it easier to write your report. And if you get confused, you can always look at your chart or list to remind yourself of what you wanted to say next.

Outline
Were Dinosaurs Warm-Blooded?

I. Scientists used to think dinosaurs were cold-blooded. Now many scientists believe some dinosaurs were warm-blooded.
   A. It still seems that some dinosaurs were cold-blooded.
   B. Other scientists believe that dinosaurs may have been neither warm-blooded nor cold-blooded.
   C. No one knows the answer to this question for sure.

II. Warm-blooded means that the body is always the same temperature.
   A. Cold-blooded animals can't keep their bodies at the same temperature all the time. Their bodies have the same temperature as the air or water that surrounds them.
   B. Warm-blooded animals are able to be very active.
   C. Cold-blooded animals are not as active as warm-blooded animals. They move more slowly and they also grow more slowly.

III. Scientists have many reasons for believing that some dinosaurs were warm-blooded. But other evidence may not support this theory.
   A. Some dinosaurs were like mammals and birds in some ways. Their legs were directly under their bodies, instead of at their sides. They

had large blood vessels in their legs, like mammals. Some small dinosaurs had large brains, like mammals.

B. Some dinosaur fossil bones have growth rings, like cold-blooded animals; other fossil bones have no rings, so maybe those dinosaurs were warm-blooded.

C. Fossil tracks show that some dinosaurs were very social and moved around in herds like warm-blooded animals.

D. Many dinosaurs walked upright; they ran instead of crawling. Running takes a lot of energy, which may mean they were warm-blooded.

E. But huge animals would have problems if they were warm-blooded. Their bodies might overheat. So some scientists think they could not have been warm-blooded. They believe huge dinosaurs were gigantothermic. This means they were similar to cold-blooded animals, but they warmed up very slowly in the sun and then cooled down very slowly at night. This would keep their body temperature more or less the same all the time.

F. Warm-blooded animals have special bones in their noses that keep them from getting dehydrated. No one has found them in dinosaur fossils, so maybe they weren't warm-blooded. But maybe the climate was wetter then, so they didn't need these bones.

IV. Scientists are looking for more evidence that will prove whether dinosaurs were warm-blooded or not.
   A. Warm-blooded animals grow faster, so scientists study dinosaur nests to find out how fast dinosaurs grew.
   B. They are studying growth rings to see if they are like the ones in cold-blooded animals today. Some people think the growth rings only tell how fast the dinosaurs grew.
   C. Scientists are searching for nose bones in dinosaur fossils. They are also looking for more information about dinosaurs' social behavior.
V. Summary: A lot of evidence seems to show that some kinds of dinosaurs were warm-blooded. Other evidence is confusing and many things are not yet known. The question won't be answered until new evidence is discovered.

CHAPTER 11

WRITING YOUR REPORT

YOU ARE NOW READY TO WRITE your report. When your teacher first talked to the class about report writing, he or she may have given you some rules about how to do it. If so, you will want to follow these rules. Certainly your teacher told you that reports must be written neatly. If they aren't, no one can read them! Using a computer, of course, makes every letter very clear. If you're writing your report by hand, take your time so the words will be easy to read.

Make sure also that you know how this report is supposed to look. Are you going to make a cover? Should you draw a map or pictures to put in it? How long should the report be? Look at the box below to remind yourself of other things your teacher may have said.

How many pages, or how many paragraphs?
If handwritten, use pencil or pen?
Write on every line (single-space on computer), or skip every other line (double-space)?
Write on one side of the paper, or both sides?
Where do the page numbers go on each page?
Where should you put your name on each page?

The sentences that are in the "conclusions" boxes at the bottom of your chart can be the first sentences, or topic sentences, of paragraphs in your report. The topic sentence gives a general idea of what that paragraph will be about. The rest of each paragraph will give details or explanations about this idea or fact.

As you write each paragraph, try to say things as clearly as you can. You want the reader to understand what you've learned about your topic. Again, pretend you are explaining it to a friend. Say a sentence out loud and then write down the words you've just said.

When you talk to someone, you use different kinds of sentences. It's a good idea to do that when you write, too. Sentences that all start the same way are boring. Make your report more interesting to read. How about beginning or ending a paragraph with a question?

When you finish each paragraph, stop to look it over. Did you say what you meant to say? Did you include everything you wanted to include? Is the paragraph clear and understandable? If the answer to any of these questions is no, now is the time to change things. There is nothing wrong with changing what you've written and redoing it to make it better. People who write books and magazine articles do this all the time.

Look back at your outline. This is a way of checking to make sure you've put in all the details you planned to. If you have, you can check off that section and move on to the next paragraph.

Here is the way one person used the notes and outline about warm-blooded dinosaurs to write a report. As you read it, maybe you'll think of ways it could have been better. Keep these thoughts in mind when you write your own report.

Each report you do will be easier to write than the one before. It will also be better. You've probably heard that "practice makes perfect," and it's true! As you practice doing research, organizing your ideas, and writing reports, you'll get better and better at it. Like playing baseball or playing the violin, writing is a skill that you can learn only by doing.

WERE DINOSAURS WARM-BLOODED?

Scientists used to think that dinosaurs were cold-blooded. Now many scientists believe that some dinosaurs were warm-blooded, but that others were cold-blooded. Other experts have a different idea. They think that maybe dinosaurs were neither warm-blooded nor cold-blooded. No one has proved any of these theories yet.

Warm-blooded means that the body is always the same temperature. Warm-blooded animals have a built-in way of keeping their body temperature even. It doesn't matter what temperature the air or water around them is. This is different from cold-blooded animals. Their bodies become the same temperature as the air or water around them.

Warm-blooded animals are able to be very active all the time. But cold-blooded animals are not. They move more slowly than warm-blooded animals, and they slow down or even hibernate when the weather is very cold. Cold-blooded animals also grow more slowly than warm-blooded animals.

Scientists have many reasons for believing that dinosaurs were warm-blooded. Here are some of them. First, some dinosaurs were similar in many ways to mammals and birds, which are warm-blooded. Their legs were directly under their bodies, instead of sticking out to the sides like alligators' legs. They had large blood vessels in their legs, similar to mammals. And some small dinosaurs had large brains. Mammals have large brains, but most cold-blooded animals have small brains.

The bones of cold-blooded animals show growth rings, but warm-blooded animals' bones don't. Some fossil dinosaur bones have growth rings and others don't. This may mean that some dinosaurs were warm-blooded and others were cold-blooded.

Other evidence that dinosaurs were warm-blooded was found in fossil tracks of large herds of dinosaurs. Social animals that travel in herds, like deer and elephants, are warm-blooded, so it's likely that dinosaurs were, too.

Fossils also show that many dinosaurs walked upright and that they could run fast. Since running takes a lot of energy, this is another reason for thinking dinosaurs were warm-blooded.

But some scientists think that huge animals like dinosaurs could not have been warm-blooded. Their bodies would have become overheated very quickly. These scientists believe the gigantic dinosaurs were gigantothermic. Like cold-blooded animals, gigantothermic dinosaurs could not keep their body temperature even. But their huge size would make them warm up very slowly in the sun and cool down very slowly at night, so their temperature would stay fairly steady.

A special bone in the nose of a warm-blooded animal keeps it from getting dehydrated or drying out in hot weather. But no one has found this bone in dinosaur fossils. This makes some scientists think the dinosaurs could not have been warm-blooded. But others think that the climate in dinosaur times was much wetter than it is today, so dinosaurs would not need this special bone.

Scientists who study dinosaurs keep looking for more evidence to prove they were warm-blooded. Warm-blooded animals grow faster than cold-blooded ones, so scientists are studying fossil dinosaur nests. This will help them learn how fast dinosaurs grew.

They are also looking at the growth rings in dinosaur bones to see if they are like the ones in cold-blooded animals' bones today. Some people think the growth rings don't have anything to do with being warm-blooded or cold-blooded. They think the rings show how fast the animal grew. But even if that is true, knowing how fast a dinosaur grew could tell a lot about whether it was warm-blooded.

Other scientists are searching for evidence that dinosaurs had the special nose bones. This would be important proof that they were warm-blooded. They are also looking for more information about dinosaurs' social behavior, to see if they acted like mammals in herds.

A lot of evidence seems to show that some kinds of dinosaurs were warm-blooded. But other evidence is confusing. It's hard to find out about animals that lived so long ago, and many things about them are not known yet. The question of whether dinosaurs were warm-blooded won't be answered until new evidence is discovered. It's a scientific mystery that might take years to solve.

CHAPTER 12

CHECKING YOUR REPORT

FINALLY YOU HAVE FINISHED writing your report. But there is one more important step before you hand it in. Checking over your report doesn't take long. And this is how you make sure that all the work you did was worth it. You've done a great job so far. Take time now to polish up your report. You want it to look its best!

Does your report say just what you wanted to say? Read it out loud, either to yourself or to someone else. You'll notice right away if something sounds strange. Maybe some of your sentences are not complete. Put in the missing words. Or you may have a sentence that seems to run on forever. Split it into two or more shorter ones. As you read, the person listening can tell you if he or she has trouble understanding any parts of your report. This will let you know that those parts need to be fixed.

Try trading reports with a friend for a final check. When you read what you wrote yourself, it's often hard to catch mistakes. After all, you know what you meant to say when you wrote it. Another person may be able to see misspelled words that you have overlooked or places where you forgot to put in capital letters or punctuation marks.

Even if you used a spelling checker on the computer, you might not have caught all your mistakes. For instance, if you typed "the" instead of "that," the computer won't know it's the wrong word. A friend who reads your report can see the problem.

Don't forget that neatness counts. If there are a lot of mistakes that you need to correct, it is a good idea to copy that whole page over if you wrote by hand. If you used a computer, fix all the mistakes and then print out the report again. When your report is neatly written, your teacher will be able to think about what it says instead of being distracted by corrections you wrote in. Look at the box below for a reminder of things to check in your report.

> Indent the first line of every paragraph.
> Begin each sentence with a capital letter.
> End each sentence with a period, question mark, or exclamation mark.
> Check your spelling.
> Check for missing words.
> Number your pages.
> Put your name on every page.

DID YOU LIST YOUR SOURCES?

Even if it's not required, a bibliography (a list of the sources you used) is a good addition to your report. It shows that you did research to learn about your topic. If your teacher told you how to make your bibliography, do it that way. If not, here is one method that many authors use:

> Author's name, last name first. "Article name (if any) in quotation marks." *Title of book*. Place of publication: Name of publisher, year of publication.

List the sources you used in alphabetical order by the author's name; if there is no author (as in an encyclopedia, for example), alphabetize by the title of the book or article. List the addresses of Internet sites just the way they appeared on the screen.

The bibliography for a report on warm-blooded dinosaurs might look like this:

Bailey, Jill, and Tony Seddon. *The Young Oxford Book of the Prehistoric World.* New York: Oxford University Press, 1995.

"Dinosaur." *Compton's Encyclopedia & Fact-Index,* Vol. 6. Chicago: Compton's Learning Co., 1994.

Lessem, Don. *Dinosaur Worlds: New Dinosaurs, New Discoveries.* Honesdale, PA: Boyds Mills Press, 1996.

Scientific American: Ask the Experts: Biology. http://www.sciam.com/askexpert/biology/biology11.htm, updated 9/97.

EXTRAS

Does your report need a cover? Would a picture help people understand what your report is about? Some reports don't need anything but words. But sometimes a good report can be even better with something extra.

Would a map be helpful? Your report might be about where dinosaur bones were found, where your grandparents were born, where you went on vacation, or where Columbus landed on his voyages to America. A map might tell more about these topics than you can say in words. Trace or copy your map from an atlas, or see if you can find one to print out from a computer. Don't forget to label any maps you add to your report.

If you found inexpensive pictures for your report at a museum gift shop or stationery store, be sure to put them in. Maybe you found a magazine picture showing something about your topic. Even clip art printed from a computer can add life to your report.

Of course, you can always draw your own pictures. Check out a library book with good illustrations. Use them as your models or trace pictures from the book. If your pictures are on small pieces of paper, paste them to whole sheets of paper so they won't fall out of your report.

A cover can be made out of almost any kind of paper. Construction paper, typing paper, and even notebook paper make fine report covers. A report on how food gets from farm to supermarket would look great with a cover made from a brown-paper shopping bag. And the cover for a report on what it's like to be a newspaper reporter could be made from the front page of your local newspaper. Paste it on notebook paper to keep it from tearing. For a report on a holiday, make a cover out of gift-wrapping paper with an appropriate holiday theme.

If your report is longer than one page, you will need some way to hold it together so the pages don't get lost. Anything that goes with the look of the rest of your report is fine, unless your teacher has told you how it should be done. You can staple the pages and cover together along the left edge, or use a paper clip. Or try tying the pages together with yarn through punched holes so that it looks like an old-fashioned scrapbook.

At last your report is ready to be handed in. It's filled with the interesting information you've gathered, as well as your own ideas. The pages are neatly written or printed out, and the spelling is correct. Everything has been checked. Be sure your name is on the cover and on every page—this is a report you can be proud of. You've created a super school report!

CHAPTER 13

RECOMMENDATIONS FOR YOUR STUDY SPACE

WRITING A REPORT IS MUCH EASIER if you have a good place to work. It doesn't have to be a whole room of your own. Maybe you share a room and a desk, or maybe you do your homework on the kitchen table. Wherever your study space is, you need:

- a smooth, flat surface to write on
- good light for reading and writing
- a chair that's the right height for your desk
- study tools, like scratch paper, good paper, pencils, pens, eraser, and ruler

With this equipment, you have a good

start on doing your best work. And of course, if there's a computer you can use, all the better.

YOUR REFERENCE SHELF

As you go on in school and do more writing, you'll want to have some reference books of your own. Maybe you already have a dictionary. Keep it in your study space so that it will be handy when you want to use it. If you don't have one, why not ask for one for your birthday?

There are other kinds of reference books that are nice to own. You don't need to get them all at once, but here are some you might want in the future. All the ones mentioned below come in book form, but many reference works are available for computers, too.

DICTIONARY

Use a dictionary to make sure you spell words correctly in your report. You can also look up the exact meaning of a word you want to use. What kind of dictionary do you need? Dictionaries that are written especially for elementary school students are easy to read and to use. The ones for older students and adults are harder to read, but they have more words in them.

A good way to pick out the kind of dictionary you want is to look at several different ones in a library or bookstore. Try looking up the same word in each one. Then you can see which dictionary's definitions are most helpful for you.

Most dictionaries also contain special features, such as maps of the world and of the United States, tables of weights and measures, and lists of facts about the presidents of the United States. Here are some dictionaries written for students:

Macmillan Dictionary for Children,
published by Simon & Schuster, New York.

Webster's New World Children's Dictionary, published by Simon & Schuster, New York.

Scholastic Children's Dictionary,
published by Scholastic, New York.

The Harcourt Brace Student Dictionary,
published by Harcourt Brace, San Diego, California.

Unabridged dictionaries (the huge ones that contain thousands and thousands of words and definitions) are expensive, but they can be a good investment. Before buying one, it's a good idea to visit a library or bookstore that has a good, up-to-date reference section. Look at the contents page to see what each dictionary contains besides word definitions.

For instance, *The Random House Dictionary of the English Language,* Unabridged Edition (published by Random House, New York) has a thirty-page color atlas; concise dictionaries of French, Spanish, Italian, and German; the complete texts of the Declaration of Independence and the Constitution of the United States; and several other extra features. *Webster's Third New International Dictionary* (published by G. & C. Merriam Company, Springfield, Massachusetts) has several useful lists, such as constellations and stars, and many color illustrations of butterflies, flags, birds, and so on. Since both have good reputations as dictionaries, perhaps your choice will be based on the extras that you think will be most useful.

THESAURUS

A thesaurus is a dictionary of synonyms. Synonyms are words that have the same or similar meanings. It's good to have a thesaurus to help you avoid using the same words over and over again. Some thesauruses are complicated to use, even for adults. Here are two that are written for students:

> *The American Heritage Children's Thesaurus,* published by Houghton Mifflin, Boston.

> *The Harcourt Brace Student Thesaurus,* published by Harcourt Brace, San Diego, California.

ATLAS

It's nice to have an atlas at home so you don't have to go to the library every time you want to look at a map. There are lots of different kinds of atlases. Some of them are very expensive. Here are three that are published in paperback and are not very expensive:

> *The New York Times Atlas of the World,* published by Times Books/Random House, New York.

> *Hammond New Century World Atlas,* published by Hammond, Maplewood, New Jersey.

Oxford Essential World Atlas, published
by Oxford University Press, New York.

ALMANAC

These books are filled with all sorts of information. Many are rewritten every year so they have all the up-to-date facts. They are usually hard to read because the type is so small, but they can be useful resources when you need to know something specific. Here are three to look at:

The World Almanac and Book of Facts
and *The World Almanac for Kids* (yearly
editions), published by K-III Reference
Corporation, Mahwah, New Jersey.

Information Please Almanac (yearly
editions), published by Houghton Mifflin,
Boston.

INDEX

report
  checking of, 75–80
  cover of, 78–80
  definition of, 6
  ending paragraph for, 64
  fastening together of, 80
  handling disagree-ments in, 57–59
  how to organize, 60–61
  listing of sources in, 77–78
  maps in, 79
  neatness in, 76
  outline for, 64–67, 70
  pictures in, 79
  quotations in, 55
  trading of, with friend, 76
  writing of, 68–74
research
  doing, 14–18
  on Internet, 29–32
  from interviews, 37, 38, 48, 49, 56
  in library, 19–28
  in museums, 33–35
  newspapers and magazines for, 36
  quotations used in, 55
  on TV, 35–36
  See also conclusions

search engines, 29–30
sources
  on Internet, 48
  listing of, in report, 77–78

See also bibliographies; research
spelling checker, 76
study space, 81–86
synonyms, dictionary of, 84–85

table of contents, 25, 27
thesaurus, 84–85
titles of books, 48, 77–78
topic
  choosing, 10–13
  different reports on same, 5–6
  should not be boring, 13
  writing about part of, 10–12
TV, 35–36, 42–43

unabridged dictionary, 17, 83–84

Web. *See* Internet
writing of report, 68–74

90

ABOUT THE AUTHORS

Elizabeth James graduated from Colorado College with a B.A. in mathematics. In addition to her books for young readers, she has written screenplays, as well as nonfiction and novels for adults. She lives in Beverly Hills, California.

Carol Barkin received a B.A. in English from Radcliffe College. Formerly a full-time editor of children's books, she now does freelance editorial work when she's not writing. She lives in Hastings-on-Hudson, New York.

Ms. James and Ms. Barkin wrote plenty of school reports and book reports when they were in school, and they have applied the methods of research and writing that they learned then to create the nearly forty books they have written together. Since they live on opposite ends of the country, their collaboration also requires a lot of organizational skills!